An Evolved Me...

Shirley Mainer

BookLeaf Publishing

India | USA | UK

Presentation by *BookLeaf Publishing*

Web: www.bookleafpub.com

E-mail: info@bookleafpub.com

ISBN: 9789358313741

First edition 2023

It's Me

Loving you is what I do,
Not in the way you want me too.
But in the way I know I can,
Because it resonates with who I am.
Look at me, who do you see?
My eyes should tell you, this is me.
I talk, I speak...
I walk, I run...
I am soaking up the sun.
I am splashing in the sea.
I am soaring through the sky.
I am praising the God, who created me.

Soon To Be A Part Of Me

He knew me before I knew him.
He made contact thru a friend.
We met, we talked
Unknowingly, I sought him and he sought me.
He was soon to be a part of me.
He said I gave too much of myself,
fight for the cause , nothing else.
I was young, what did I know,
Of the things you hold and the things you let go,
Of the things you nurture and the things you let
die,
Of the things you keep and the things you pass
by.
He'd been around he was marked, too,
But there was another side of him to see,
Which was soon to be a part of me.

LIFE

Sometimes it's hard and
we don't understand.
The idea of living seems not so grand
But always remember yesterdays,
are our eyes for tomorrow
and our tears for today.
Because we are not moving by
just our thoughts and ways.
So look at life through your eyes and mind.
There you may see things that are great.
Surprise!

Free

Free to laugh!
Free to cry!
Never, never free to lie.
Free to walk!
Free to run!
I was once your number one.
Honor, Trust, Respect...
All the things I would expect.
Nothing more, nothing less!
Nothing left but regrets.
Do I forgive,
Do I forget.
Grace and Mercy
Have set me free.

LIVING

5

Life is for living.
Breathing, Being, Seeing...
Life is for living.
Learning, Laughing, Longing, Loving...
Life is for living.
Giving, Growing, Getting, Grateful...
Life is for living.
Pleasing. Pausing, Praying...
Life is for living.

My Child, My Love

6

They say she has my eyes.
They say she has my nose.
They say she has my lips and the smile I hold.
But when I look in the mirror at me,
I never see what they see.
I am running from reality.
As long as her heart is filled with love,
She will always be a gift from above.
She will always be my child, my love.

Waiting on Wisdom

I don't know,
I should
I've lived a life of
would, should and could.
Would if I could,
Should if I could.
But would I know if I....
I don't know,
I see.
I've lived a life of
being and seeing.
Even believing in the unseen.
I don't know.
I want to know.
At what point do I know that I know,
do I know that as I grow,
I have become WISE...

Today

Sitting, watching the sunset.
Slowly, slowly it goes down.
I'm reflecting on today's ups and downs.
I began with a stretch.
Then a leap out of bed/
Then a prayer for a peaceful sleep! Grateful!
Then a prayer that will guide me thru the day!
Hopeful!
Then a prayer that will guide me thru the ups
and downs.
For not many days go all one way.
What can I say?...Today was...
So tomorrow once again,
I will pray for another Today.

Words

9

Spoken words are expressed everyday
Some softly, some loudly.
Some lyrically, like in song.

Unspoken words are unexpressed,
buried so deep, so as to forget.
When it's time they tumble out,
regretfully, with pain which
has been suppressed, controlled.
Words are to be told...Let them go!

Creation

Closed eye imagery
I see, I see it visually.
Get busy hands, creativity
Get busy hands reality.
No longer an impossibility
It was made by me.

SMILE!

So you say I do not smile.
Just wait a minute, wait a while.
I don't know you, you don't know me.
I may not be who you think you see.
I may want you to just let me be.
I may have just walked a mile.
I may have just failed a test.
I may be unduly stressed.
I may just be one big mess.
I may just need some time to rest.
Just wait til you see me at my best.
Then I'll show you my biggest smile.
Just give me a minute, wait a while.

Looking Back

I've been a child.
I've been a sister.
I've been a friend.
So many memories of who I've been.
I've been a student.
I've been a teacher.
I've been a leader,
So many memories of what I've learned.
I've been a daughter.
I've been a wife.
I am a mother.
So many memories of them in my life.
That's how I define me.
That's who I am, when I look back.

Because I love you!

Just because I love you,
I had to let you know
I am in awe of you
I am so proud of you
As I've watched you grow.
Let me tell you this,
while it's on my mind.
Don't take for granted any day.
Live your life in real time/
Make the best of everyday.
Find happiness in your own way.
Your are loved.

Leaving

I want to leave gracefully.
Having watched the journey end,
I want to smile peacefully.
No regrets, no sorrows,
No wishing for more tomorrows.
Even in darkness, I can see light.
Feeling brightness within sight.
Ready to soar to new heights.
Ready for a new life.
Not looking back on what was left.
No need to remember the nights I had wept.
Preserving what goodness I have left.
Moving on to discover my new best...

Free...Water

Floating, such a free feeling,
Closing my eyes, letting go.
free, free, free...

Standing in the shower,
feels like rain, be still,
free, free, free...

Swimming in the pool,
Close my eyes, kick, kick, kick,
stroke, stroke, stroke, float, float, float,
free, free, free...

Swimming in the ocean,
feeling the waves.
sending me in, then out again
sending me in. then out again.

The water is my happy place,
Where I can be free, free, free...

Dark Days

Some days seem really dark.
Please don't let the darkness in.
Don't even think those thoughts.
Let's just say the day is dim.

Walking in negativity
Attracts it more and more..
OMG, when will this end.
Here comes one hit, then another
How much more am I to suffer.

Light at the end of the tunnel...
Light at the end of the tunnel...
Am I getting any closer?
What the heck is wrong with me?
It's not even that bad...
I just remembered who I BE.
Then I lit the light in ME.

Goodbye! Friend?

No, No, No,
Why would I assume so?
Here it is in black and white.
Does that make it right?
Think about it, read it again.
Ok, Ok,
Now I pick up my pen,
I'm gonna tell you exactly what I think.
That stuff you are saying really stinks.
Why? Why?
Would you tell such lies?
When did your sense of decency die?
Tell me! Tell me! Tell me again!
No, No, No,
We can't be friends.
Honesty, trust and loyalty are important to me.
You mess up one...You lose all three!

Pleasure

Sweet, salty, savory
Tasty treats for sure.
Some are so so pleasing,
I keep going back for more.

Springtime smells, shady trees.
Simple pleasures more of this please.
As I sit and enjoy an afternoon breeze.

Simple pleasures, hardly any stress.
Soaking up the sun, getting my best rest.

Travelling to far away places,
Every night a different dream.
Longing to make more memories.
Longing for things yet unseen.

In SILENCE

I hear the bird sing.
I hear the wind ring.
I hear the raindrops.
I hear the tick tock of the clock.
I hear the buzzing of the fan.
I hear the foot tap.
I hear the hand clap.
I hear the finger snap.
I hear a laugh.
I hear a moan.
I hear the ringing of a phone.
I hear my thoughts.
I hear the beat of my heart.
I hear SPIRIT saying "BE STILL".

WHY

Why do I do what I do?
Why do I say what I say?
Why?...is the question everyday.
As I rise...
Why am I here where I am?
Why do I wear what I wear?
Why do I sit here and steer?
At this life...
Why do I go where I go?
Why don't I know, what I don't know?
As I think...
Why do I move like I move?
Why do I groove like I grove?
The only reason seems to be,
Because I can.

FAITH

21

F eeling
A s
I f
T ime
H eals

F ollowing
A ll
I nformation
T hat
H eals

F orming
A lliances
I nterestedly
T hinking
H eal me!

F inding
A ll I need
I s the one that
T ruly
H eals!